The Two Nichols:
Spent for Missions

The
Two Nichols:
Spent for Missions
JESTER SUMMERS
Illustrated by Dick Wahl

BROADMAN PRESS
Nashville, Tennessee

2823

© Copyright 1982 • Broadman Press.

All rights reserved.

4242-79

ISBN: 0-8054-4279-0

Dewey Decimal Classification: J266.092

Subject headings: NICHOLS, BUFORD//NICHOLS, MARY FRANCES//
MISSIONS—INDONESIA//MISSIONS—CHINA

Library of Congress Catalog Card Number: 81-70910

Printed in the United States of America

Thank You

To Mary Frances and Buford, The Two Nichols
To Katherine Cook and the Baylor University
  Program for Oral History
To Catherine Walker and Kirke White of the
  Foreign Mission Board, Richmond, Virginia
To The Kimble County Museum and The Kimble
  County Library, Junction, Texas
And to Ray Summers, a valuable consultant

—for helping to write this book.

Contents

About Mary Frances Hodges:
Not Yet One of the Two Nichols

Home on the Ranch

"Wake up, children!" Mr. Hodges called from the kitchen door. "It's moving day."

Mary Frances opened her eyes and rolled out of bed at the same time. So did her older sister, Aleen. They could hardly believe it. The long-awaited day had come.

After breakfast, both girls watched as their two older brothers and Mr. Hodges loaded everything the family owned on the wagon. Papa swung five-year-old Mary Frances and Aleen right up on top of the mattresses. The boys climbed on by themselves. Mama sat on the spring-seat.

"Nettie," said Mr. Hodges to his wife as he climbed in beside her, "we are really going to our own home on our own ranch at last."

Mama looked happier than the girls had ever seen her when she turned and warned, "Girls, lie very still now. I don't want to lose one of you."

They stayed as still as they could. But it was not easy to do, riding for two miles over a very rough and bumpy road.

At last, the wagon stopped, and Mary Frances looked out. She could see only the roof of the house and porch. "Oh, Aleen," she squealed, "look how big the house is! Does it have an upstairs?"

Both girls scrambled off the wagon and ran into the empty front room. They "Oh'ed" and "Ah'ed" when they saw the fireplace. "It's just like the one Grandma Hodges has," they

9

exclaimed, clapping their hands. They forgot all about the upstairs—which the house did not have.

They checked out the fireplace room and the kitchen of the new log home. And then Mary Frances said, "Let's go see the pine room!" And the two rushed out the front door, off the porch, over the rock patio into the pride of Mary Frances' heart.

This room made her feel special. She was the first of her family born in it. Papa had built the addition next to their first log house, which was on his mother's land, before Mary Frances was born. Recently, he had moved the pine room to the new location by putting it on wheels pulled by horses and mules.

While Mary Frances and Aleen were looking at the pine room, Mama and one of the brothers brought in a large wash-tub and set it in a corner. It was covered with a pretty quilt.

"I know what's in there," Mary Frances said as if she were the only one who knew the secret.

"I know, too," countered Aleen.

"Cakes," Mama Hodges said. "Twelve cakes for Christmas. And I know you won't bother them."

And they didn't. Somehow it made them feel good inside when they obeyed Mama and Papa Hodges.

At Christmastime each year, Papa's family brought food for a big dinner together. On another day, the Millers, Mama's family, did the same. There was boiled ham, baked chicken, and roast beef or steak and gravy. And, of course, all kinds of pies and cakes. But when anyone would ask Mary Frances what she wanted to eat, her father would answer teasingly, "Give her meat and more meat. That's all she ever wants." Mary Frances did like sweets. But Papa was right. She liked meat best of all.

On this Christmas after the "move" both the Millers and the Hodges had their special dinners in the new home. And that's when the twelve cakes were eaten. Of course, the cousins came with the aunts and uncles. And there were so many of

10

them that the children had a great time playing games. They played hide-and-seek, little-white-house-over-the-hill, and blindfold. They also sat on a huge log down by the Llano River just below the house and watched the wind make ripples on the water.

"I had a good time today," Mary Frances announced after the company had gone.

"We all did," the family decided.

School at Gentry Creek

"Mary Frances, stay close to Aleen at school today," Mrs. Hodges advised her seven-year-old daughter. It was Mary Frances' first day to go to school as a pupil.

Mother handed her a lunch pail and explained, "You are going to like what is in this bucket—ham in biscuits, fried sweet potatoes, and an apple."

Mrs. Hodges lifted a somewhat frightened and silent daughter into the saddle in front of Aleen. "Old Sorrell is a gentle horse," Mrs. Hodges said. "But you will ride her slowly, won't you, Aleen?" Aleen promised.

Just to make the trip a bit safer, the older brothers walked ahead as the girls rode along behind. The one-room schoolhouse was about a mile away, near Gentry Creek on the main road to Junction.

After attending school for several weeks, Mary Frances began to see words she knew in her reader. "This is May. How do you do, May? This is Spot. How do you do, Spot?" she read. She especially liked the pictures of Spot. Mary Frances liked dogs!

Recess was fun when they all played "steal-the-rock." As Mary Frances grew older, she learned to streak across a middle line, steal a rock from the other side's rock pile, and dash back to her side without being caught.

Mary Frances liked to study geography because in it she learned about people and places far away. "I want to go to other parts of the country when I get older," she thought.

11

When Mary Frances was about ten years old, Mrs. Hodges announced to the family one day, "I have good news for all of us. Beginning next Sunday at three o'clock there will be Sunday School and preaching at the Gentry Creek schoolhouse every week. And all of us are going."

"Papa, too?" the children asked.

"Papa, too!" Mr. Hodges replied.

Mary Frances and Aleen loved the Bible stories they heard and read at Sunday School. Each week they received a card with a Bible verse on it. And if they had memorized that verse by the next Sunday, they were given a new one. Mary Frances and Aleen learned many, many verses over the next year or two.

Finally, the Sunday School leaders said, "We should give these young people Bibles for their good work." And they did. For the first time, Mary Frances had a Bible of her very own. It was little and black, and a complete surprise!

The people of the community decided one summer to ask Brother S. F. Marsh to preach for them every night for a two-week revival. He agreed. The men put up posts on the school yard. To the top of the posts they nailed boards. Over the boards they laid brush, twigs, and leaves gathered from the bushes growing along the creek bank. Benches were brought from the schoolhouse and lamps from homes. This was called a "brush arbor." It made a cool place for morning and evening worship services.

One night Brother Marsh, who was staying with his wife at the Hodges' home, made an announcement. "Each evening," he explained, "I am going to assign you a chapter in the Bible to read." Then he added, "And Mary Frances Hodges will keep a record of those who read the chapters each day. If any of you cannot come to the night service, but you have read the assigned Scriptures, call Mary Frances and let her know."

This kept Mary Frances busy for the whole revival. Young people, who had to miss a service, would call her to report and learn what to read the next day. She loved it all. More than that, she began a habit of reading her Bible daily.

After the brush arbor meeting was over, the people asked Brother Marsh to preach for them one Sunday a month. He said he would be glad to come. Many of his sermons were on Paul's missionary journeys. And along with the Bible thoughts he told stories about missionaries who were serving in places like Africa, China, and South America. Mary Frances listened carefully to this preaching. She thought carefully about what the preacher said.

Something Special

Mary Frances and three of the older children were teenagers when Mr. Hodges bought a Model-T Ford. During the next spring, all four of them drove into Junction for revival services. At one of the meetings, the preacher spoke on "Jesus the Savior." For a year or more Mary Frances had been thinking, "Why don't I give my life to Jesus? I want to do so, very much." While the preacher continued, she decided, "I will do it now." During the invitation she went forward to make her decision known. The feelings of guilt and loneliness she had felt left her, and a quiet peace came into her heart. She was baptized as a believer on the next Sunday afternoon in the nearby Llano River. She had joined the church where Brother Marsh was pastor.

In the days that followed Mary Frances began to think, "Jesus has done so much for me. He is my Savior. I want to do something special for him all the rest of my life."

A Narrow Escape

Mary Frances and Aleen finished the ninth grade at Gentry Creek School. They started going to high school in Junction. They drove to town in the family Model-T. That is, Mary Frances did the cranking to start the motor. Aleen did the driving. The town wasn't too far away, about eight miles. But the roads were unpaved and often rough and filled with ruts, especially in bad weather.

13

On their way home from school one afternoon after a heavy rain, the two girls stopped at an uncle's house to ask about crossing the river up ahead. Their uncle went with them to check. The low-water crossing was already covered. "I think you can make it just fine," said the uncle. Aleen drove carefully through the water. But just as they pulled out of the deepest part, a huge tree rushed over the crossing just behind them.

For a few minutes, both girls, usually talkative, were silent. "That was a close call," they decided. All day, both were nervous about their narrow escape. "The Lord spared us for some reason," Mary Frances kept saying to herself. That night two grateful girls read their Bibles and thanked God that nothing tragic had happened.

College and a "Call"

Two years later Mary Frances graduated from high school. She gave the prophecy for her class. It was a speech in which she predicted, for fun, what each class member would do and be in the future. This was her very first time to speak in public. She rather liked doing it. She said afterward, "I'm going to marry a blue-eyed, black-haired man who can speak in public."

Both girls wanted to go to college. But the family had little money to help them. "I'll tell you what we can do," one sister said to the other. "We can work this year, save our money, and go to college next year." This plan worked out well. Mary Frances lived with a ranch family near Menard, Texas, and taught their six-year-old daughter to read. Aleen worked and saved her money, too. And the next fall they went to the College of Industrial Arts for Women in Denton, Texas, nearly three hundred miles northeast of Junction.

On their first day there, as they were signing up for freshman courses, Mary Frances saw a table with these words over it: "If you wish to take a course in Bible, sign up here."

She nudged Aleen and said, "Look over there. Let's take

15

that Bible class." Aleen liked the idea. Miss Mabel McQueen, a former missionary, was the teacher. She taught Matthew the first term. The class studied John the next time. Throughout the two courses, Miss McQueen told of her experiences as a missionary. And Mary Frances began to think, "I would like to be a missionary, too."

Then one day in the college chapel service, she heard this announcement: "If anyone of you is interested in doing foreign mission work, meet in the council room after supper tonight."

"I'm going," Mary Frances declared then and there.

She attended the meetings regularly. And, in the summer, she was sent to the convention of International Student Volunteers for Foreign Missions which met in Detroit, Michigan. Experiences at that meeting made her more certain than ever that God was calling her to be a foreign missionary.

"And the place is Africa," she decided.

After she finished college at Denton, she was hired to teach art in one of the grade schools in Austin, Texas. However, when Mary Frances moved to Austin in the fall, she had no idea what exciting things were about to happen in her life.

About Buford: The First One of the Two Nichols

"Boys, Keep the Law!"

Buford, the first of the two Nichols in this story, was born on a farm in east Texas, near Milam. The land bordered on the Sabine River, along which many large trees grew. As a small boy, Buford loved to sit on the riverbank and listen to the wind moaning through the tall pines, oaks, and hickories.

Of course, this was not all Buford did. Farming many acres of land kept the family working hard from early morning till sundown. But no matter how late it was or how tired they were, the family routine always ended with a short worship time. Papa Nichols would read a few Bible verses. Then both parents prayed. Mama Nichols, in her prayer, would mention the names of the nine sons and one daughter. And Buford, even when tired and sleepy, would try hard to stay awake until he heard her call his name. Somehow, this made him feel good inside and safe.

One day, Mr. Nichols came home from Milam rather upset. At supper, he told the family why. "Today, I saw a man erasing marks on a postage stamp so he could use it again," he explained. "That is dishonest!" he declared, "and against the law."

Not long afterward, Mr. Nichols took the boys to the jail in town to let them see the prisoners behind bars.

"Look at the expressions on their faces. Not one of them is happy," whispered Papa in a sad voice.

Next, he took them into an empty dark cell and closed the

17

door. They could not even see their own hands. "Boys," Papa said kindly, "keep the law. Don't bring disrespect to the flag. Honor your country and be proud you are an American! You don't ever want to be put into a place like this. Be honest."

Buford seldom found it hard to obey his father. Papa made it pleasant to do so, though the object lessons he used in teaching were sometimes unpleasant experiences. The dark jail cell was one of those. But Buford never forgot it or his father's exact words.

Hailstones, a Brickbat, and Rattlesnakes

Mr. Nichols moved his family from the damp river valley of East Texas to a flat, dry farm near Sweetwater in West Texas. Buford was nine years old at the time.

That spring while he was chopping weeds in the cornfield, a storm came up quickly. Buford ran for the house with a roaring wind chasing him. Just when he thought he was winning the race, hailstones began falling all about him. They pounded out craters in the freshly-plowed ground. They stripped twigs and leaves from the mesquite trees as he ran through the pasture.

More than once he stumbled over the rolling ice "missiles." But he won the race, with few bruises. Later a neighbor, whose mule had been killed during the storm, picked up a hailstone that barely fit into a gallon syrup bucket.

"I could have been killed!" Buford thought.

That night the family thanked God that Buford was saved from injury or maybe death.

Not long after this, Buford and several of his brothers were helping Mr. Nichols round up and pen several skittish horses. One of them dashed for the open gate as Buford ran full speed to close it. At the same moment, Mr. Nichols threw a broken brick to head off the horse. The brickbat missed the horse and landed on Buford's head. It was two days before he knew what had happened.

For the second time that summer, Buford realized how narrowly he had escaped death.

On a cloudy day near the end of that season, Buford and his older brother, called S.B., were playing in a nearby gourd patch. They were watching bullbats, or nighthawks, buzzing and diving high above them. And they weren't looking where they stepped.

Suddenly, Buford felt a squirming, wriggling something under his bare left foot. Before he could put the other foot down and leap for safety, he heard a frightening rattle. He could feel the snake's fangs sink into his heel as he jumped to run. The snake held on for several steps before Buford could shake it loose.

The two boys raced for the house a hundred or more yards away. S.B. ran right on through it and down to a neighbor's house to call the doctor in Sweetwater.

"You've been bitten by a rattler!" exclaimed Mama as she saw the blood spots on the floor.

"A sharp stick, Mama," Buford said, not wanting to frighten his mother.

But when she saw him tying a cord tightly around his leg below the knee, she knew the truth. Quickly, she mixed salt in kerosene and put his foot in it to soak. Finally, Buford said to Mama, "Well, a little old rattlesnake did sort of bite me." Mother had said nothing. She just kept on stirring the salt and kerosene around his heel.

Buford's conscience began to bother him. And so he told her the truth about the rattler attack.

The doctor in Sweetwater kept a car ready for speedy runs in that "rattlesnake capital of the world." Almost as soon as S.B. called him, he was on his way! He soon passed Mr. Nichols, who had heard about it and was driving homeward as fast as his horses could run.

Later after the doctor had given the anti-snake-venom shot, and he was feeling better, the doctor talked with him. "Little

20

man, you saved your life by tying that cord around your leg. Where did you learn to do that?"

"About two weeks ago," Buford answered, "I was walking around the front of our house and heard men on the porch talking, and I listened. They were explaining to each other what to do for a rattlesnake bite."

That night at prayertime, Buford's parents thanked God that their son had been saved that day from death. And Buford added, "Saved the third time this year!"

New Life and a "Call"

When Buford was about fifteen years old, the family moved back to Milam in East Texas. Buford started going to Bethany Baptist Church where many young people attended. "Most of those are Christians," he thought, "and they live their lives as I want to live mine. They go to worship services and enjoy it. I'm going to do that, too." And he became one of them. But he was not yet a Christian.

The summer Buford was seventeen, he attended all the revival services in the little town, as did the young people who were his friends. He listened to the sermons night after night and kept asking himself, "Why does a good person need to become a Christian? I'm not bad. I've done nothing wrong that I know of."

One morning as he was helping his mother with the chores, she said to him, "Buford, you are a good son. I hope you will trust Christ as your own personal Savior."

That night just before the service began, Deacon Joel Halbert came over to him, shook his hand and spoke words from his heart. "Buford, you are such a good boy that you really ought to be a Christian. God loves bad people, so he surely loves a good boy like you."

Later, the pastor explained Jesus' death on the cross this way: "Christ died for all—the bad and the good."

"That makes sense," Buford thought. "Jesus makes bad

people good. And he makes good people better. That's what I need: to be better." He started to go forward and make his decision known. But just then he saw Mama. "If I go now, she will shout. That will be embarrassing." So he waited. But he didn't wait long, for when the people began to sing "I Will Arise and Go to Jesus," Buford did just that.

Sure enough, Mama did shout and praise God. But he was not embarrassed at all. In fact, he felt such a peace in his heart that he wanted to shout, too.

Two weeks later, Buford attended a study led by Mr. J. H. Bunch from Dallas. This teacher spoke often about telling others of Christ. He explained how God calls people to be missionaries. At the end of the study, Mr. Bunch asked, "If anyone of you feels that the Lord is calling you to be a missionary, will you come and stand by me?"

Buford, and at least a dozen others, went forward.

When Buford reached home, two miles from town, Mama greeted him with a hug and kiss. She had heard what he had done. "I thought this was going to happen," she explained. "I feel that the Lord is going to use you in a wonderful way."

To College on Twelve Bales of Cotton

Before Buford's last year in high school the family moved to Beeville, Texas, where Buford became very interested in going to college. He played football and basketball. He debated and entered speaking contests and won awards in both. And he began to dream of being a teacher or preacher. The call to missions had faded.

It was about this time that the Beeville school superintendent said to Buford, "You ought to go to the best university in Texas next year."

"Where is that?" Buford asked.

"The University of Texas in Austin," came the reply.

Buford thanked Mr. Madarra for his encouragement. But he wondered, "Where will I ever get enough money to go away from home to school?"

He graduated from high school in the spring. And he decided that where there is a will to do something, there might be a way. With this in mind, he looked for and found work. From July till December 20, he picked twelve bales of cotton around Beeville, Roby, and Hamlin, Texas. That was enough cotton-picking to pay for his first year in the University of Texas.

In December, Mr. Nichols moved his family to Austin, the best move the family ever made. He began working as a gardener on the grounds of the state capitol. He later became the head gardener of the capitol greenhouse, a position he held for the rest of his life. And Buford was able to stay at home while getting his degree.

"My going on to school is just like a miracle!" he concluded.

"Not a Buffalo Nickel"

On Probation

In January, Buford went to sign up for study in the University of Texas. The registrar counted his high school credits. Then she said, "I'm very sorry, but you have only fourteen. We require sixteen credits to enter school here."

Buford just stood there, stunned and speechless.

The registrar saw his shocked look and said she would check his high school records again. She did. "I have it!" she exclaimed as she checked one more time. "Because your grades were so high, I can give you one credit for quality. And with fifteen credits you can enter on probation."

"What does that mean?" Buford asked.

"It means that you will have to make good grades in all your first term classes," she answered.

He did make good grades. He studied hard. And because he liked to learn about many subjects, he enjoyed doing it.

During that year, Buford joined the nearby University Baptist Church. Soon, they asked him to be pastor of one of their missions in northwest Austin.

The next year two small churches called him to preach for them one Sunday a month each. And he began to feel the Lord wanted him to be a pastor. He really enjoyed preaching. And he liked working with the church people.

"She Is Different"

Soon after school started in the fall of 1928, Buford attended a college "Get-Acquainted Party" at University Baptist Church.

It so happened that Mary Frances Hodges, just out of college in Denton and teaching in Austin, had joined the same church. And she was at the party, too. Neither knew the other until two lines were formed opposite each other. Men stood in one and women in the other. The lines marched in opposite directions, stopped at a signal, and persons in one line shook hands and got acquainted with those directly across from them. After several such stops, Buford found himself shaking hands with a very striking young woman.

"I'm Buford Nichols," he stated, "not a buffalo nickel. However, that may help you remember me and my name."

It did. Mary Frances laughed. "He is clever," she thought, "and nice-looking. too." She told him her name, and they talked for a while. He decided right there, "She is different from all the other women I've met. I would like to know her better."

Soon after the party, interested students were invited to teach in the mission Sunday School on the northwest side of town. When Mary Frances heard the announcement, she said to herself, "Why, I can begin doing mission work now." And she volunteered. Then she learned that Buford Nichols was pastor of the mission.

Decorating the Christmas Tree

One Sunday night about Christmastime Buford made this appeal at church, "We need volunteers to help decorate a tree for the mission Christmas party. Come this next Friday at seven o'clock if you can help."

Mary Frances was the only person who responded. The two did not mind. They had a wonderful time making and putting colored paper chains on the tree. They strung red and green ropes here and there around the room. And, of course, they talked a lot.

By the end of the evening, Buford had made up his mind. "She is the one for me!" he had decided. However, he said nothing about it at that time.

Back at the church soon afterward, he looked at her information card in the college Sunday School files. When he saw that she was planning to be a foreign missionary, he thought, "Perhaps, I had better not get too interested in her. I'm feeling now that God has called me to be a pastor, not a missionary."

Nevertheless, Buford began to walk Mary Frances home from prayer meeting on Wednesday nights. Several times he tried to call her for dates. But she was always out. Finally, late one Friday, he found her at home. She told him she was very sorry, but that she could not see him that night. She just felt that she was too tired to talk much and, besides, her hair wasn't freshly washed—reasons she did not explain to him, however.

Buford did not give up. He kept seeing her after prayer meeting on Wednesdays.

On Valentine's Day, Mary Frances received a pretty card with a heart on it from Buford. Thinking that he had probably sent one to the other Sunday School teachers at the mission, she walked up the street to see one of them.

"A valentine from Buford came today," she began. "I'm sure you received one, too."

"Of course I didn't," replied the friend. "Mary Frances, don't you know Buford Nichols is in love with you?"

Well, she hadn't known it. But she was more than pleased that she just might be his best girl.

When the Baptist church at Round Rock called Buford as pastor, the University Church ordained him to the ministry. He was surprised and pleased when he saw Mary Frances in the audience for the service. From then on he called and saw her more often.

"How Can I Let You Go Without Me?"

In the spring of that year, Buford said to Mary Frances, "I'm graduating from university this May. I'm going to Fort

Worth to Southwestern Seminary in June. Why don't you go there for the summer term?"

Mary Frances thought about the idea for some time. Finally she concluded, "To study there will help me prepare for mission service." So she attended the seminary that summer.

She taught in Junction in the fall and winter and lived at home on the ranch. Buford made several trips to see her and came to love the ranch country as she did.

In August, Buford arranged for Mary Frances to teach young people at a church encampment held at Driftwood on Onion Creek near Austin. He was the camp pastor.

After church one night, they talked a long time about their plans for the future. Buford asked Mary Frances if she still felt God was calling her to be a missionary to Africa.

"At this time that is the plan I feel God has for my life," she replied.

"But, Mary Frances," Buford objected, "How can I let you go without me? I feel that God wants me to preach, not to be a missionary." Dejectedly he added, "I guess we can't be married even though I feel God sent you my way."

Finally, they decided to pray about it and left it at that. Both were sad as they parted after the camp ended. He went back to seminary, and she taught school again near her home.

Two Nichols for One

The Problem Is Solved

Mary Frances and Buford kept writing to each other. And they kept praying that God would help them know what they ought to do. Then, in a flash, one day, the answer came to Buford. "Why, I can preach in Africa or China just as well as I can here in the United States if that is what the Lord wants me to do."

He went to the ranch at Junction in Kimble County to see Mary Frances. He shared his decision with her. Mary Frances agreed happily that they could leave the future to the Lord's leadership. They decided to marry after her school term ended in January.

An Unforgettable Day

The date for a church wedding was set. The details were planned. And on Sunday morning at 9:30, February 15, friends and relatives from all over the county filled First Baptist Church at Junction. They listened joyfully to the ceremony that made "Two Nichols" instead of just one.

As the service ended and the bride and groom left in the Model-T, it began to rain. It kept pouring all that day and night as a friend drove the couple to Fort Worth, 250 muddy miles away. Most of the roads were unpaved. Some were not graveled either. The car stuck in the mud now and then, but the men managed to get it out.

At dawn the next morning the couple arrived at their apartment at the seminary. A neighbor couple, the H. D. Bruces, invited them to breakfast. "How wonderful," the two Nichols exclaimed. "We accept. We are starved!"

For Buford and Mary Frances, February 15 became a wonderful, unforgettable day in spite of the rain and hunger.

And Then There Were Four

Four years of living at the seminary passed quickly. Mary Frances took several Bible courses. Buford finished his doctor of theology degree, taught at the seminary, and pastored a full-time church in the city.

During that time Buford Lee, Jr., and John Conner were born. And then there were four Nichols instead of two.

"Called" to China

Appointed as Missionaries

"Dr. Nichols, I have something I want you to do for me," said the seminary president one day in the spring of 1936. "Two men from the Foreign Mission Board in Richmond, Virginia, are coming here for a one-day visit. They want to talk with each of our mission volunteers. Will you set up a schedule of conferences with the students for that day?"

"I will be glad to do so," replied Dr. Nichols.

On the appointed day he met Dr. Charles E. Maddry and Dr. R. S. Jones at the train. All day he saw that the two men and the volunteers had their meetings together. At the end of the day, Dr. Maddry asked Buford to join them for a visit. After a few words about the day's conferences, Dr. Maddry said, "Now, how about you, Dr. Nichols?"

"What do you mean?" Buford replied.

"We want you to volunteer, too," was Dr. Maddry's reply. "Seminaries are needed in five countries where we have mission work," he went on to explain. "We need to train the men in those countries whom God calls to preach and teach."

"And we feel God can use you to help start this work," Dr. Jones added.

"I don't think I could go right now," Buford hedged.

"Talk it over with your wife. Think and pray about it. And then let us know," the two men urged. Buford promised he would.

That night he told Mary Frances of the challenge for them

33

to be missionaries, perhaps to China. Mary Frances was ready to say, "Let's go. I'm ready." But she waited for Buford to feel the same way. After several weeks of praying, they decided together that God was renewing the call he had made to both years before.

Buford wrote their decision to Dr. Maddry.

In October, they went to Richmond to be appointed by the Foreign Mission Board. "We want you to go to North China first," they were told. They agreed.

Eleven other volunteers were appointed for China at the same service.

The Missionary Voyage Begins

In December, the four Nichols sailed out of Vancouver, Canada, on the British Ship, *Empress of Russia*. The eleven other missionaries sailed on the same ocean liner. On the way, twelve of the group were very seasick. But Mary Frances was not one of them.

They sailed in sight of Alaska and the Aleutian Islands. While docked in Japan for loading and unloading, they made a trip to see famous Mount Fuji.

At last, the ship sailed into the Shanghai port. "Mary Frances," Buford said, "here is where our missionary voyage really begins."

They stayed for a few days in Shanghai. While they were visiting the Baptist University there, Chinese Christians gave Buford a new name: "Nee Bee Lee."

The "Nee" was Chinese for Nichols. (The surname is placed first in China.) Then "Bee" for Buford came next. And "Lee," his English middle name, was last.

On to Peking

"First, you must learn the language of your new country," the Nichols were told when appointed. "You must be able to preach, teach, and talk with the people."

Thus, they went next to Peking to study in the language

school there. After the four were settled into an apartment, school began for the parents.

"Oh, this is hard and tiring," they said. "Just to listen to the teacher say the same word over and over and repeat it after him over and over gets tiring."

But they reminded each other that "this is a part of God's call. And he cannot use us here until we can talk with the people."

With this reminder they felt better and gave their best effort to the study. While the Nichols were in Peking, Japan made war on China.

Home in Hwanghsien (HWANG-shin)

After more than a year's language study, it took the Nichols six months to get permits to travel north. Buford was assigned to teach in the Shantung Seminary located in Hwanghsien, North China. This he did for about a year.

The family enjoyed living there on the mission compound. Their house was next door to the home of Dr. and Mrs. W. B. Glass. "They are grand neighbors," the Nichols often said. They enjoyed fellowship in the compound with the Charlie Culpeppers, the Frank Lides, Dr. and Mrs. N. A. Bryan, Wilma Weeks, Martha Franks, and Anna Hartwell.

"The Big Red Houses"

But the time had come for the Nichols to move to a new place. They had gone to China to help begin an all-China Baptist seminary. The place chosen for it was Kaifeng (KĪ-foong) in inland Honan Province.

So they packed their things and traveled several days by boat, ship, and slow train. On the way, they passed through country already captured and occupied by the Japanese army. However, they had no trouble. That was in 1939.

When the crowded train reached Kaifeng, no one met the Nichols. Buford could see several large foreign-looking red buildings not far from the station. "I know that is the mission

36

compound," Buford said to his family.

To a rickshaw man he said, *da hung chia,* and pointed toward those "big red buildings." The man understood. He and other rickshaw men took the Nichols and their luggage straight to the mission.

When the Nichols arrived, the missionaries were surprised to see them. For some unknown reason, they had not received telegrams or letters about the Nichols' coming. The people of the mission apologized for not meeting the train. And then they gave all four newcomers a warm, hearty welcome.

During the next several months, Dr. Nichols helped start the all-China seminary in the Bible school building, one of the *da hung chia.* It opened with ten students and four teachers. Buford was beginning the work he had been "called" to China to do. And so was Mary Frances. She taught in the Baptist girls' school in Kaifeng.

The Double Dragon Street Baptist Church

Dr. Nichols not only taught in the seminary full time, but he also pastored churches in and around the city. One of these was the Double Dragon Baptist Church. It took its strange name from the street on which it stood.

One Sunday morning at this church, Dr. Nichols preached on the subject "Christ Died for Our Sins." Several came at the end of the service to confess their sins and seek Jesus as their Savior.

One very old woman came hobbling down the aisle on her bound feet. She fell down on her knees and hands in front of the pulpit. And, as she did, she exclaimed, "If this Jesus died for my sins, as you say, I want to give him *kowtow* [KO-toe]."

The Christians rushed to her and helped her stand. They said, "We do not bow nine times to Jesus as the idol worshipers do!" And they explained how she could become a Christian. To *kowtow* was the only way the old woman knew to give highest honor to Christ.

Another elderly woman who attended that church, came to

38

Buford with a request. "I want to enter the school where the children go," she stated.

"That wouldn't do," she was told. "You would be sitting on little stools among pupils who are only eight to ten years old."

"That would make no difference to me. And I can bring a larger stool if I need it. Please let me study in this school," she pleaded.

Dr. Nichols then asked, "Why, at your age of sixty-one, do you want to learn to read and write?"

She pointed to his Bible on a nearby table, and she said, "I did not know there was a book like that. Lately, I've been hearing people read and talk from it. And I see some of these children carrying it in their hands. I'd like to learn to read it for myself."

The school board did not grant her request. But a group of ladies from the Double Dragon Baptist Church went to her house and taught her to read from her own Bible. And she started carrying it wherever she went.

And Then Came the Japanese

Honan Province fell to the Japanese. They ruled in Kaifeng. Although they kept a close watch on the mission compound at all times, they made little trouble for the missionaries and what they were doing. That was, of course, before they started war against the United States.

But some of the Chinese seminary students did not fare so well. One young minister and his wife went to a Japanese clinic, as they were ordered to do. The husband objected to the dirty needles they were using to give shots for contagious diseases. He was arrested on the spot and questioned. As he stood before them, he failed to take off his glasses. They knew he was aware that to enter the presence of a high officer, he should salute, take off his glasses, and bow. So they knocked his glasses off and started making trouble for him.

"You are a rebel. You are a spy," they accused.

He was wearing a Western-style suit. So they asked, "What are you doing here?"

He said, "I'm in school."

"And what do you study there?" they wanted to know.

"The Bible. I am a Christian minister," was his reply.

"Oh, you are? Well, you are going to have to give up your religion," they commanded.

"My father and my grandfather—my whole family—are Christians. I cannot give it up," he answered. "It means more than life to me."

The officials put an iron rod in a coal-burning stove. "We are going to heat this iron and use it to make you say, 'I give up my Christianity,' " they shouted.

They did burn his hand. They even threatened to stick the hot iron through his hand. But he continued to say he could not give up his religion. All the while, he pleaded with them to let him go and prayed that God would help him to stay loyal.

Suddenly, they put the rod down.

"Well," they said calmly, "if you feel that way about your religion, you must really be a Christian and are not here spying on the Japanese. You may go home." They put medicine on his injured hand and let him go.

Dr. Nichols and the other missionaries had heard about the student's arrest. The whole mission station prayed for him during the awful ordeal.

The Japanese war in China grew worse. The missionaries of Kaifeng received a message from the United States government. It read, "For their own safety, American women and children should leave China at once. We cannot be responsible for them."

The Nichols prepared to obey, as did two other missionary families with children. Uncertain times had come to the seminary and the mission work in Kaifeng.

The First Trip Home

An Early Furlough

Dr. Nichols took his family to Shanghai soon after the message came from the United States Embassy. He put them aboard the American ocean liner S.S. Washington and watched them sail away toward the United States.

He went back to Kaifeng to spend a lonely Christmas with other missionaries whose families had also gone home. He continued to teach in the seminary the rest of the spring. But the threat of war between Japan and the States was growing. Already World War II had started in Europe.

Since Buford's furlough would soon be due, it was decided that he should go home early. So he joined his family in June. And after a few months in Junction, Texas, they went to Fort Worth where Buford taught in the seminary for a term. During that time, David Hodges Nichols was born.

The attack on Pearl Harbor happened during that time, too. And the United States was at war with Japan.

Before the year was over at the seminary, Buford said to Mary Frances, "We won't be able to return to China as a family until the war is over. What would you think about our going to the University of California at Berkeley? I can take a master's degree in Oriental languages." And he added, "I need more skill in speaking Chinese." Mary Frances was glad to go. And the family was soon off for a year in California.

One to China and Four to Texas

Furlough time was up for Buford. He took his family back to Junction, Texas, and he returned to China. But this time, he

41

went in from India to the western part where the Japanese had not yet invaded. With other missionaries already there, he preached and ministered to Chinese retreating from the on-coming enemy armies.

Mary Frances and the boys stayed in Junction until they found a house in San Marcos, Texas. Buford Lee, Jr., and John Conner attended the Sam Marcos Baptist Academy not far from where they lived.

As the Christmas season drew near, the boys wanted to know how they would spend the holidays without their daddy.

"We will go to the ranch as soon as school is out," Mary Frances told them, "and we will stay till New Year's Eve." This pleased the children, for they loved to go to Grandmother Hodges' house. Thinking about the coming vacation made the time pass more quickly for the boys. But not hearing from Buford made it very slow for Mary Frances. She had received no word from him since Thanksgiving.

Finally, the last day of school came, and the four Nichols packed up their clothes and gifts and drove to the ranch, eight miles north of Junction.

Grandmother Hodges knew they were coming. And as soon as they had unloaded the car and taken off their wraps she brought out food she had prepared just for them. From the warming ovens of the wood stove, she took homemade bread, ham, chicken, and other foods the boys liked. From the icebox she got cold milk, butter, and a vegetable salad. And, of course, there were dozens of Grandmother's sugar cookies for dessert.

Christmas Eve and Christmas Day passed far better than Mary Frances expected. As usual, they had the Hodges' family dinner, and later the Miller family get-together. The children had fun with all the cousins, just as Mary Frances had done when she was growing up on that same ranch.

To the Top of Tea Cup Mountain

Mary Frances and the boys spent the last days of the year in the woods and hills. They picked up pecans, set traps for ringtails, rode horseback. They went to bed every night literally exhausted.

One morning, they decided to ride over to Tea Cup Mountain, several miles across the valley.

"Let's climb to the top today!" one boy said.

"That is a great idea!" the other replied.

Their mother thought so, too. And as soon as the three of them could put on warm clothes, they started for the barn. They saddled two horses. One was very gentle. The boys mounted him and started slowly for the road. The other was gentle, but spirited. He had been trained as a cutting horse, a fact that had slipped Mary Frances' mind. She soon remembered, however. The minute she put her left foot into the stirrup, the horse was off like a shot. She held on for dear life and finally got her right foot into the stirrup on the other side. All the while she was shouting "Whoa!" Of course, as soon as she was able to pull up on the reins, the horse stopped. This was just the way a cutting horse was supposed to act. For a minute she sat to catch her breath and to sigh a prayer of thanks that she had been spared from a possible tragedy. Then she trotted out of the corral, down the road to the meadow, and joined the boys.

When they reached the foot of the mountain, they dismounted and dropped the horses' reins. Carefully they climbed from rock to rock, right up the mountainside. At the top they sat down and looked out over the land in all directions.

To the south, they could see the town of Junction. On the east side, they located the Hodges' ranch house and the Llano River. To the north was the Reichenau Mountain Pass on the Old Beef Trail. Through it, in the early days, cowboys had herded thousands of cattle on their way from South Texas to Dodge City, Kansas.

On the west were mountains too high to see beyond, even from the top of Tea Cup. The three climbed down the mountain and found their horses just where they had left them.

44

"These horses have moved only a few feet from where we dropped rein," observed Buford Lee, Jr., in wonder.

"They have been trained to do that," answered their mother.

On the last day of 1943, the four Nichols returned to San Marcos. Their drab, old house was cold, and the firewood was wet. It took an hour or two to get the place warm.

Saturday was New Year's Day. Mary Frances slept late, and so did the boys. "It will be another sad day for us, I'm afraid," she thought as she woke up at nine o'clock. But just then the telephone rang. "Buford!" she said as she jumped out of bed and ran for the telephone. She lifted the receiver, answered, and heard the operator say, "I have an overseas cablegram for Mrs. Nichols, please."

With her heart pounding, she listened to the message: "Arrived in Bombay. Buford L. Nichols." That was all the operator said, but it was enough.

"What was it, Mother?" shouted three wide-awake youngsters.

"Daddy is safe in Bombay!" she answered in a very happy voice. She had not told them that for the last month or more their father had been on ships moving through waters infested with German and Japanese submarines.

They built a roaring fire and had a wonderful time together on that first day of 1944!

Saved by a Sermon

Settled in Shanghai

The war finally ended in 1945. Dr. Nichols came home and stayed for about a year. Then he and his family returned to China, but not to Kaifeng. By then, the Chinese Communists ruled that city, and no missionaries were allowed in that part of the country.

The all-China seminary that had been in Kaifeng was opened in Shanghai. Its classes were taught in the Baptist university of that city. Dr. Nichols was one of the teachers and at times acted as head of the seminary.

Mary Frances taught art and English in the Eliza Yates Baptist High School.

The Communist armies continued to take province after province in the northern, eastern, and southern parts of China. They continued to move westward until they finally marched into Shanghai. The Communists hated Americans. And so, for sixteen months, all the missionary families, including the Nichols, were under house arrest. They could not leave the mission compound or go anywhere without permission from the Communist guards.

The Christian Chinese could have little to do with the missionaries because it brought suspicion and danger to them. The Communists took over all the Baptist schools and managed them. They placed spies in each class. Guards were nearby at all times. As a result, fewer and fewer Chinese were brave enough to attend classes.

The Nichols sent Buford Lee, Jr., and John home to the United States in the summer of 1949. But Mary Frances was not allowed to take David and leave at the same time. They did not know why.

The Long, Brown Envelope

One day, about six months after the two boys left, a Communist messenger rode into the mission compound on a bicycle. He strode into the seminary building calling out, "Nee Bee Lee!" He had a long, brown envelope in his hand.

Dr. Nichols stepped out of his office and walked down the hallway to meet the official. He took the envelope and signed for it. He opened it and read silently, "Appear in court for trial tomorrow morning at nine o'clock." That was all.

During the hours that followed, and far into the night, brave Chinese friends and pastors came to encourage and support him. However, one man offered this strange advice: "It will be best for you to sign anything they ask you to. I know of people who have survived by admitting crimes they did not do." Buford decided right then he would not follow that suggestion.

A pastor explained that one of his church members might be on the panel of trial judges. "If so," the pastor explained, "he will let you know by giving a sign with the fingers on his left hand. Or, if he is not there, another judge will make the sign or you will see a very faint smile on his face."

Next morning, Buford left the compound with a sinking feeling. The day was February 15. It was his and Mary Frances' nineteenth wedding anniversary. Death or long imprisonment could separate them forever. Fear gripped him. But at the same time, he was praying, "Your will be done, O Lord. I'm in your care."

At the courthouse, an usher silently took him to a seat near the front of a large room. He sat in the dim light for a long time, alone. The long, brown envelope was clutched in his
48

hand. He had no idea why he was there, nor what the charges would be.

After a while, two men, who seemed to be court lawyers, entered the room, stiff, stern, and silent. They sat on the top tier of seats directly above and in front of Buford. One of the men held in his hand a sheaf of papers. Later, he came down and compared his papers with those in the brown envelope and kept both.

Next came six judges. They sat three in a row just below the two lawyers and squarely in front and above Buford.

Buford watched for a left-hand sign from one of the six men. But he saw no familiar hand movement at all. One judge did seem to force a tiny, leering smile just for a slight second. "Perhaps," thought Buford, "this man knows someone who knows someone who knows me. That may help." But, of course, he was not sure.

At last the man with the papers and the envelope came down from the top tier. He stood before Buford and began to read aloud. He named all the crimes the seminary professor was charged with doing. As he read page after page, his voice got louder and angrier. "You are a spy," he yelled. "You are against the poor and oppressed workers!"

His closing charge was that Buford had fired a grass cutter at the mission compound without enough pay to keep his family until he could find other work. "And you refused to rehire him when he could not find another job."

Sometime back, Buford had heard about the firing after he returned from a trip inland. The man had been dismissed because he would not do the work.

Then the lawyer accused him of killing the grass cutter's father years before Buford even came to Shanghai. The father had fallen off the top of a train he was riding and had been killed. "Your mission is responsible! That man was working for you when his death occurred."

"Life for life! Death for death!" the lawyer shouted as he walked up and down between the judges and Dr. Nichols. He

stopped. Dead silence followed. One of the judges pointed his finger toward the missionary and cried, "I recommend death for you. You are a murderer!"

The judges then went to a side room. And after much loud talking and arguing, they returned. The spokesman for the group gave the verdict.

"This man is guilty." He paused, then added, "The penalty for this crime is death."

He handed the written verdict to the silent lawyer who had been watching Buford through the whole trial. He rose and asked Buford, "Do you have anything to say?"

After a brief pause, Buford stood calmly and quoted this verse in Chinese, "For God so loved the world, that he gave his only begotten Son, that whosoever believeth in him should not perish, but have everlasting life" (John 3:16). From this he preached quietly for about fifteen minutes on God's redeeming love through Christ's death.

As Buford began to speak, some of the men were making loud remarks to him. But as he continued they quieted, and soon all eight of the men seemed to be hearing what he said.

As he finished, a soft silence filled the room. The judges looked at one another. And then they returned to the side room. Once again, they argued loudly. Afterward, they came out and talked in low voices with the lawyers. When they had finished, the chief lawyer stepped down before Dr. Nichols and said, "If you will give this offended family eighty million yuan [yu-AN] (Chinese dollars), we will let you go free."

"I have very little money," the missionary replied. "I get only enough to care for my family monthly. But I can go to my mission, not far from here and see if they can help me in this matter." He added, "I hope someone is there at this hour on Saturday afternoon."

Answered Prayers

An armed guard went with Buford to the mission office. All the way, Buford kept asking himself, "Will Frank Connely be there at two o'clock on Saturday? He seldom is. And will he have eighty American dollars in Chinese yuan?''

But Frank was there! He threw his arms around Buford saying, "I was afraid I would never see you again. The Lord still answers prayer."

Buford explained what he needed. "We have some cash," Frank answered, "but I'm not sure we have that much on hand. And the banks are closed on Saturdays."

Fearfully, they opened the safe and began to count the money. When they had finished, they looked at each other in amazement. "Eighty million with hardly one yuan over!" "The Lord used his Word to bring a miracle," said Buford. "The sermon and money are of the Lord."

What a happy time followed! People everywhere were saying, "Praise the Lord. He answered our prayers."

"I'm going to make my life count more for Christ from now on," was Buford's promise.

Mary Frances Decides

Soon after Buford's trial Mary Frances announced to him: "A live missionary is worth more to the Lord's work than a dead one. I believe the Lord is telling us that it is time to leave." The remaining missionaries felt the same way. So, after filling out government forms for six months, they finally received permission to return to the United States.

After fifteen years of missionary service in China, the Nichols left that field for good.

Two Nichols for a Seminary

Off to Indonesia

"Mary Frances, how would you feel about going to Indonesia to help begin a new seminary?" Buford asked one day. They had been back from China for several months. Buford was teaching at Baylor University while waiting for the Lord to lead them to their next field of service.

"Why do you ask?" Mary Frances wanted to know.

"I have heard from the Foreign Mission Board, and they are eager to promote the training of preachers in the islands of the South Pacific." Then he added, "They want us to take the lead in starting a seminary over there."

The two of them looked at all the materials about Indonesia sent to them from the mission office in Richmond, Virginia.

The more they studied, thought, and prayed about it, the more they felt the Lord's leading.

"Well, I am for starting the seminary!" said Mary Frances. "That makes two of us," replied Buford, enthusiastically.

By November 1952, the two Nichols and ten-year-old David were taking their first overseas plane trip. They had gone by ship to Hawaii. From there, they flew to Japan, on to Singapore, and finally to Jakarta, Indonesia.

However, they went by car to Bandung [BAHN-doong], about 120 miles up in the hills. The Nichols, in their "land of beginning again," were strangers to the people, the language, the customs, and to the hot, moist climate of the equatorial zone.

Buford did not wait this time until he could speak the language to begin talking with people. He used what he called the "signs and wonders" system. "We make signs," he explained to an American friend, "and the people wonder what we mean. But it is better than not trying to get acquainted at all."

David, their young son, made friends with many children in the neighborhood. They liked to come to his home. "With so many boys and girls coming in and out, why don't we start a Sunday School for them?" Mary Frances asked. And Buford thought that a good idea.

Dr. and Mrs. Nichols and David invited all the boys and girls in their community to their home on Sundays for a special get-together. Miss Nettie Tobing, a young Christian woman, told Bible stories to the children in their own language and helped them memorize Bible verses and sing new songs. How those Indonesian youngsters loved to sing!

Then, all of a sudden, the boys and girls stopped coming. Dr. Nichols learned that the Muslim leaders had objected to the parents permitting their children to attend. He went to the village chief and explained just what the children were learning. "We love these boys and girls and only want to help them," he stated. The village chief decided it would do the children no harm and told the parents as much. Soon, the backyard was full of children, and the Sunday School was going again.

"Choice at First Sight"

Nine months after the Nichols arrived in Bandung, they were speaking the Indonesian language. And Buford began to search for the right place to build the new seminary. He flew twenty-four times to Semarang [se-MA-rang] trying to find land there for seminary buildings.

"Semarang, the capital of the Central Province of Java [JA-va], is the best place to build a school for preachers," Buford decided. And for that reason he did not give up when people refused to sell land for it. He just kept looking.

One hot April day he was riding in an old taxi along the river in western Semarang. Suddenly he said to the driver, "Stop! I want to get out here."

He started up the mountain near the side of the river and liked what he saw. But halfway up he knew he could not make it all the way to the top that day. He had a plane to catch back to Bandung.

The first thing he did the next time he landed in Semarang was to head for the low mountain and climb to the top. One look was enough. The view from there was breathtaking. "This is it!" he exclaimed. "This is the spot I've been looking for!"

Later, he told his co-workers, "It was choice at first sight." The Foreign Mission Board gave its approval for buying four acres on the mountaintop. As soon as the plans were completed for the first building, work on it began.

Three months afterward, a "first-class miracle" happened. Three temporary buildings had been finished in record-breaking time. And the *Seminari Theologia Baptis di Indonesia* opened with twelve students.

Many things were lacking on that first day of school. The kitchen was not finished. So they had to bring cooked food wrapped in banana leaves from a downtown cafe for the students' meals. During the first seven months, they hauled drinking water from the professors' homes in the city. For lights at night, they used kerosene lamps and tallow candles. "We were a hardy bunch of pioneers," Dr. Nichols said of the teachers and students.

Soon after the Nichols moved into the city below the seminary, several young people came to see Mary Frances.

"Mrs. Nichols, will you teach us to speak English?" they asked. She liked the idea. She had loved working with teenagers ever since she was converted years before in Junction.

"Yes, I'd be glad to do it," she replied. Then she had a new idea! "Why don't you preach in English to the group next Sunday?" she asked Buford.

He consented at once. The young people liked it and wanted him to do it every week, which he did gladly.

From this new venture, Buford thought of something else to do. "Let's advertise the services in the newspaper and invite anyone who wishes to come," he suggested.

"Fine," replied Mary Frances, "and be sure to say it will be in English." This they did.

Eleven of the young people began to study conversational English in the Nichols' home every week. They liked to visit with David, too. He was about thirteen years old at the beginning of their class. He lent them his books, his magazines, and even his comic books. They came often to play volleyball and other games in his backyard. The group increased. At many times, the front yard was a sea of bicycles.

Mary Frances started regular meetings for them on Sundays in her living room. She cut up old quarterlies and gave each a part to study and then to tell at the meetings. This gave them a chance to read and speak English. And at the same time, they were learning Bible facts and truths.

Before long, a Baptist church was organized. And it started in the Nichols' living room.

Now, during all this time Mary Frances had school for their son, David, at home. At the seminary on the mountaintop, she taught such subjects as story telling, English, missions, and the history of Sunday School.

After Eighteen Years

For eighteen years these two Nichols spent their missionary efforts planning, building, and teaching at home, at church, and at the seminary.

When time came for the Nichols to retire, 175 of the young people with whom Mary Frances had worked in those early years came back for a reunion with her and Dr. Nichols. Seminary personnel and teachers and prominent pastors and leaders of the city honored them with farewell dinners, parties, and gifts.

One of the eight brick buildings now standing on the beautiful four-acre campus was named *The B. L. Nichols Building*.

59

A Message from and to the Two Nichols

And the Lord has led us all the way!
From the ranch home in West Texas,
And the farm home in East Texas;
From college, university, and seminary;
From pastorates and teaching tasks in Texas;
To fifteen years of preaching and teaching in China;
And eighteen years of teaching and preaching in Indonesia.
All the way we have felt his definite call
And it has led us to stay
Through hard times,
And joyous times,
Through dangerous times,
And victorious times.
He has been with us and kept us in all places
Wherever we have gone.
What a call!
What a Savior!

And our answer is: You have shown us a wonderful Lord.

Thank You, Mary Frances and Buford Nichols!

Remember

What helped the two Nichols become Christians?

How did Mary Frances become interested in missions?

When and how did Buford first feel "called" to be a missionary?

Why do you think Buford said to Mary Frances: "I'm Buford Nichols, not a buffalo nickel?"

What problem did Buford and Mary Frances have with their plans for the future? How did they settle it?

When did Buford realize God wanted him in mission service?

Why do you think they never gave up being missionaries? Was it always easy? Was it always safe?

What did David, the youngest son, help begin in Bandung? In Semarang?

Now, do you know what a "call" is—the kind that Mary Frances and Buford felt? Think about it.